More Fun With I...

Key Stage One/Primary One/...

Contents

Page

Teacher's notes

How to use this book	2
Getting started in the classroom	2
Evaluation sheets	2–3
Notes on individual worksheets	3–6
Additional activities	6
Home/school activities	6–7

Worksheets

1. Letter string 'ir' as in 'first' (1)
2. Letter string 'ir' as in 'first' (2)
3. Digraph 'oo' as in 'boot' (1)
4. Digraph 'oo' as in 'boot' (1)
5. Magic 'e' as in 'gate' (1) *
6. Magic 'e' as in 'gate' (2)
7. Magic 'e' as in 'bone' (1)
8. Magic 'e' as in 'bone' (2) *
9. Magic 'e' as in 'time'
10. Digraph 'oo' as in 'book'
11. Diphthong 'ai' as in 'rain' (1)
12. Diphthong 'ai' as in 'rain' (2)
13. Diphthong 'oa' as in 'coat' (1)
14. Diphthong 'oa' as in 'coat' (2)
15. Diphthong 'ou' as in 'found' (1)
16. Diphthong 'ou' as in 'found' (2)
17. Letter string 'or' as in 'fork' (1)
18. Letter string 'or' as in 'fork' (2)
19. Diphthong 'ow' as in 'brown' (1)
20. Diphthong 'ow' as in 'brown' (2)
21. Letter string 'air' as in 'hair'
22. Digraph 'aw' as in 'straw' (1)
23. Digraph 'aw' as in 'straw' (2)
24. Diphthong 'ow' as in 'blow' (1)
25. Diphthong 'ow' as in 'blow' (2)
26. Wh – questions as in 'what'
27. Letter string 'tch' as in 'witch' (1)
28. Letter string 'tch' as in 'witch' (2)
29. Open 'a' as in 'bath' *
30. Letter string 'er' as in 'fern'
31. Digraph 'ea' as in 'teach'
32. Letter string 'ear' as in 'dear'
33. Silent 'k' as in 'knee'
34. Opposites – time words
35. Position words
36. Alphabetical order *
37. Anagrams
38. Compound words (1)
39. Compound words (2)

Page

Teacher's checklist	47
Pupil's own checklist	48

(*Ask the children to stick the worksheet onto stiff paper or card before starting)

Teacher's Notes

How to use this book

This book offers a wide range of language activities for children working at Levels 2 and 3 of the National Curriculum in English. It covers all the English Attainment Targets. This book constitutes a progression and therefore would also be of use in Key Stage 2. The activities will encourage children to talk about words and to play with and manipulate them in a variety of enjoyable ways.

The worksheets are intended for active learning through doing and talking, which is how young children learn naturally. Children will be involved in cutting and sticking, assembling puzzles, following mazes, solving crossword puzzles, breaking coded messages, solving anagrams, rhyming, discovering word patterns, making word wheels, making up compound words, and of course reading and writing. In this book the phonic concepts covered are more advanced than previously (e.g. dealing with magic 'e', silent 'k', more digraphs and diphthongs).

Although the worksheets are progressively more difficult it is not intended that children work their way through all the worksheets in order. Rather it is expected that the teacher will select the most appropriate worksheet for the child's current needs. Some worksheets belong together in content, however, and are best done together.

The worksheets supplement any classroom programme of language teaching, whatever the approach. Children can work individually or in pairs, or a whole group could be introduced to a particular worksheet together. Ideas for extension work and homework are given separately after the individual Teacher's Notes.

Getting started in the classroom

Some of the worksheets may fit into a particular class topic the teacher has planned (e.g. Worksheet 27 on 'Halloween', Worksheet 34 on 'Time') but many are intended to be 'pure' word study. Nevertheless it is important to place them into a context which gives them meaning and relevance for children. When a particular letter string, digraph or diphthong is introduced children should be encouraged to work orally or perhaps with magnetic letters before they consolidate this learning with the worksheets.

When introducing a worksheet it helps to read through the instructions with the children before any cutting-up or writing is done. For more of a challenge children could be asked to read the instructions by themselves before reporting back to an adult on what they are required to do. This is good training for planning their actions. On many sheets it is appropriate to complete the tasks orally first – this is not cheating, merely avoiding frustrating confusion. This applies particularly to children with special needs or those who are learning English as their second language.

Some worksheets will need to be pasted onto stiff paper or card first to strengthen the final product. These are indicated with an asterisk on the Contents page. Children might also require pencils, coloured pens, scissors, split pins, glue, dice. Children who are less well coordinated may need assistance with some of the cutting-out.

Many activities lend themselves to collaborative work with a partner. Careful thought needs to be given to the pairing-off of pupils (perhaps a less-able child paired with a more capable 'tutor' or pairing two children of similar ability?) to make the task fruitful. In working with a partner children will develop their oral language and also come to a deeper understanding of word study than they might do on their own.

Evaluation sheets

The *Teacher's checklist* enables teachers to record details of pupils' achievements with the activities. It is not intended as a comprehensive checklist of all the worksheets but, rather, draws out key skills together with broader abilities. There is an intended progression in the checklist elements from left to right, as there is from the checklist elements in Book 1.

The *Pupil's own checklist* allows children to reflect on the work they have covered and to record their personal achievements themselves. This ties in with the good practice of pupil conferencing and records of achievement going on in many schools. The *Pupil's own checklist* also gives children the opportunity to share their achievements with peers, parents and other teachers.

Notes on individual worksheets

(*Ask the children to stick the sheet onto stiff paper or card before starting)

1 *Letter string 'ir' as in 'first'*
The children could highlight all the 'ir' strings they can find by circling or using a light coloured felt tip, to make the string visually stand out more. They could also write out pairs of words which rhyme.

2 *Letter string 'ir' as in 'first' (2)*
This follows on from Worksheet 1 and puts the words into the context of whole sentences. Children could work in pairs as this is a problem solving activity where collaborating with a partner would be fruitful.

3 *Digraph 'oo' as in 'boot' (1)*
Ask the children to identify the pictures first to avoid any false tracks (e.g. snoop, stoop, swoop). To make the task easier, write some letters into the crossword before the children start.

4 *Digraph 'oo' as in 'boot' (2)*
This is a comprehensive wordsearch with words arranged horizontally and vertically, but not diagonally. To simplify the task, cross off some of the words from the list, as the puzzle can look quite confusing in its latter stages – a challenge to some children of course.

5 *Magic 'e' as in 'gate' (1)* *
It might help to make the hole in the disc first. Children will need an introduction to the magic 'e' rule first to make this activity meaningful. A small group of children could produce a giant version for class display and use.

6 *Magic 'e' as in 'gate' (2)*
Children will gain more from this activity if it follows a thorough introduction to magic 'e'. Children are given pictorial clues and definitions to work out the answers. You may wish to draw a box around the target words to make them clearer. Solutions: 1. Frame, 2. Gate, 3. Plate, 4. Brake, 5. Blade, 6. Game.

7 *Magic 'e' as in 'bone' (1)*
This activity allows for plenty of extension work. The children could write lists of words and nonsense words, distinguishing them by giving definitions for the real words or drawing pictures to go with them. This could be accompanied by looking them up in dictionaries to help decide whether they are words or not.

8 *Magic 'e' as in 'bone' (2)* *
This activity is mainly oral with some purposeful reading. To make it more fun invite nonsense sentences or untruths (e.g. dogs don't like bones). Encourage children to discover for themselves what the word pattern is. They could also make pairs or triplets of words that rhyme and perhaps even write simple rhyming poems.

9 *Magic 'e' as in 'time'*
Children could be asked to find more words of the i-e pattern which rhyme with some of the given ones. This worksheet could be completed with a partner to encourage collaborative problem solving.

10 *Digraph 'oo' as in 'book'*
Get pairs of children to compare their completed crosswords and come to a consensus over any differences. Discuss clue number 7 with them – a different word pattern but it still rhymes.

11 *Diphthong 'ai' as in 'rain' (1)*
Point out to the children that the pairs of words should rhyme. They could go on to make a poem (verbally or in writing) using one of the pairs. Before completing the trail it may be useful to go through the definitions verbally with the children and to ensure they write the words in the correct space.

12 *Diphthong 'ai' as in 'rain' (2)*
Get children to make up their own clues to swap with their friends for them to draw. Ask the

children to read the completed words so they have to think about the words. Ask them to find rhyming pairs and write the complete words out again as a pair. Children could be invited to write the words in alphabetical order, too.

13 Diphthong 'oa' as in 'coat' (1)
In the first puzzle there is no requirement to also make words that read vertically - but some children might savour this particularly demanding challenge! In the last activity, children could be asked to mark the 'oa' string in some way to emphasise the visual pattern.

14 Diphthong 'oa' as in 'coat' (2)
This is mainly a reading rather than a writing activity. Working with a partner would encourage lots of discussion. Children could be asked to highlight the 'oa' pattern in all the words they find on the page by circling or underlining the string. This sheet could be contrasted with other work on o-e, where words sound the same but follow a different phonic rule (e.g. Worksheets 7 and 8).

15 Diphthong 'ou' as in 'found' (1)
This activity makes very tangible the fact that words or spellings are visual by relating them to other visual patterns. Before writing, ask the children to discover the visual pattern in the coded words and perhaps circle it.

16 Diphthong 'ou' as in 'found' (2)
To make this activity easier for children, write more of the missing letters into the crossword. Go through the clues with the children first. Children could use a dictionary to check up on spellings or could swap their completed puzzle with a friend to compare results. An 'ou' word bank might also be a useful resource to draw on.

17 Letter string 'or' as in 'fork' (1)
Identify the pictures first to elicit target vocabulary (i.e. not pig or bird). Invite children to highlight the 'or' string to make it more obvious. This activity could usefully be done with a partner.

18 Letter string 'or' as in 'fork' (2)
This activity follows on from Worksheet 17 and it would be helpful to allow the children to draw on their little booklets for the spellings. Alternatively they could try them themselves and then check with a friend or a dictionary. Ask them to list rhyming pairs, too.

19 Diphthong 'ow' as in 'brown' (1)
Get children to highlight the 'ow' string in the wordlist. To make the activity easier write some of the missing letters into the crossword for the children. This sheet lends itself to collaborative problem solving with a partner. Children could check the spellings with a dictionary and also compare definitions. There are no vertical words. Contrast this activity with Worksheets 15 and 16 – same sound, different spellings.

20 Diphthong 'ow' as in 'brown'(2)
Ask children to highlight the 'ow' string in all the words on the page. They could also list rhyming pairs and make short poems from them.

21 Letter string 'air' as in 'hair'
To make this activity easier you could write some of the missing letters into the puzzle before giving it to the children. Children could use an 'air' word bank to draw on or they might create one after completing the activity. They might like to use a dictionary to check spellings or compare definitions.

22 Digraph 'aw' as in 'straw' (1)
This activity also focuses attention on word spaces, a frequent source of conflict between teachers and pupils! The task at the bottom puts the words into meaningful context. Children could make up little poems verbally or in writing, using some of the rhyming words found.

23 Digraph 'aw' as in 'straw' (2)
Children could check their spellings with a dictionary or by swapping with a friend and comparing their attempts. The second task could be simplified by removing some of the given words or extended by adding more. It could be started off in school and finished off as homework.

24 *Diphthong 'ow' as in 'blow' (1)*
Contrast this activity with Worksheets 19 and 20 (same spelling, different sound) but avoid presenting the two different 'ow' sounds together at first as it would lead to confusion. Children could make up their own rhymes using 'ow' words.

25 *Diphthong 'ow' as in 'blow' (2)*
For the first activity, two words have to belong to the same family – e.g. blow and blown. The children find the odd one out.
Solutions: 1. snow, 2. crow, 3. blown, 4. slow. The second part is very useful for work on word endings (-s, -ed, -er, -ing).

26 *Wh- questions as in 'what'*
In preparation for this activity children could be invited to compose wh- questions orally. Point out the use of inflection in oral language and the equivalent of a question mark in print. As an extension children could search through some story books for question marks and see which words these sentences start with.

27 *Letter string 'tch' as in 'witch' (1)*
This activity is more fruitful if children have already been introduced to the 'ch' sound, so that this becomes an extension. To add more meaning to this task ask the children to write a story about a witch using as many of their 'tch' words as possible.

28 *Letter string 'tch' as in 'witch' (2)*
The fact that spelling patterns are visual is made very tangible by relating them to other visual patterns. Before they write, prompt the children to discover by themselves the visual pattern to the coded words.

29 *Open 'a' as in 'bath'* *
To aid meaning you may wish to draw lines from some of the illustrations to the corresponding words. Spellings could be checked with a dictionary. Children could write a short story involving some of the words and store them in their baskets.

30 *Letter string 'er' as in 'fern'*
Guide children to discover that the 'er' string usually appears at the end of words and then encourage them to make up other 'er' words (N.B. job titles often have 'er'). Get children to circle all the 'er' strings on this page after completion.

31 *Digraph 'ea' as in 'teach'*
This is another suitable activity for work in pairs. Watch out for unfamiliar vocabulary (e.g. leap, east). It is a good idea to read through the 'ea' words first and perhaps get children to give verbal definitions.

32 *Letter string 'ear' as in 'dear'*
Ask children to follow the maze first with their fingers. Words on this worksheet could be contrasted with other words following the same spelling pattern but sounding different (tear, wear, pear) and words sounding the same but written differently (e.g. beer, deer, cheer, here). This can be quite complicated so is perhaps best aimed at more able pupils.

33 *Silent 'k' as in 'knee'*
A neater result will be achieved if children copy out the story onto another piece of paper, replacing the drawings with the target words. Ask them to cross the used 'k' words off the list. Children generally find the concept of silent 'k' quite difficult to grasp and will need to do some preparatory work before attempting this worksheet.

34 *Opposites – time words*
This activity would fit well into a topic on 'Time' or 'History'. To introduce this activity use non-time words as examples of opposites. The sheet finishes off with a nice open-ended task. Possible words: evening, clock, timer, minute, last, fast, etc.

35 *Position words*
Second language learners will find this activity particularly helpful. It would be beneficial to have a practical session first in which prepositions can be explored verbally. Encourage children to use the right vocabulary themselves. This page could also be used as an assessment tool to find out which prepositions children have in their repertoire. Do ensure that they bring you their own work and not a helpful friend's!

36 *Alphabetical order* *
This activity helps children to develop the skill required for finding words in dictionaries. It addresses not only the first letter but also the alphabetical order within words. To prevent children completing this page 'blind' (i.e. without reading the words) go through all the words with them first. Additionally you could require them to make up sentences putting some of the words in context. Watch out for unfamiliar vocabulary (e.g. cape, eel).

37 *Anagrams*
If you provide access to magnetic or other 3-D letters children will be able to arrange and rearrange them to help find the new words. This is an excellent activity for reinforcing the concept that new words can be made from old words and that it is possible to assess visually the likelihood of a spelling being correct.

38 *Compound words (1)*
The concept of compound words is not as easy as it looks as it is not immediately obvious why some words are joined together (teapot) while others are not (shoe laces). Children also need to have a firm grasp of word spaces before attempting compound words. An attractive display of the completed flaps could be made if they are first pasted onto card. Other easily-drawn suggestions: milkman, armband, necklace, butterfly.

39 *Compound words (2)*
This worksheet relates to Worksheet 38 but, here, children are required to partition a compound into its constituent parts. It might help to give children a small piece of masking card to slide along the word from left to right until the first word appears. This activity helps tremendously with reading by looking for words within words, a good attack strategy for unknown words.

Additional activities

Pupils will gain the most from the activities if they are embedded in the wider context of the language study going on in any classroom. In addition, there are many ways in which the work on the worksheets can be extended and enriched, as suggested below.

To put the study of individual words and word patterns into a more meaningful context children could be asked to write a whole sentence or short story using one or as many as possible of the words from the sheet. Many worksheets require children to do this already, but this extension is suitable for practically all the pages.

Instead of writing sentences or stories children could be invited to compose rhymes involving words from the worksheets. Initially these could be simple two-liners, later progressing to longer prose. You could add an element of fun by asking for nonsense or silly poems. The rhymes could be made up and presented orally or in written form as a further extension.

Alongside any activities on detecting and producing rhyme (a significant indicator of success in reading) children could also be involved in auditory discrimination activities. These are particularly good for developing listening skills. Choose some of the words from the worksheet and some that are not on the worksheet (three or four altogether) and say them slowly one after the other. Children have to identify the odd-one-out (e.g. Worksheet 5 hate, mate, rope). Difficulty can be increased by making the odd-one-out more similar to the others (e.g. hate, mate, cape).

Games are always a highly motivating way of reinforcing teaching points. The kind of track game featured on Worksheet 8 can be adapted to provide extra practice for any words the teacher selects: they could be words from the class topic, words following any other letter pattern, thematically grouped words (e.g. days of the week), etc. A group could be involved in creating a larger, sturdier version of the game for class use.

Home/school activities

A number of the worksheets lend themselves to forming a link between home and school. This might be by simply being taken home and shared with family members, or being used for extra practice or as an extension for related activities. Some of the extension activities in the 'Notes on individual worksheets' would also be suitable for homework.

The word wheel on Worksheet 5 or the track game on Worksheet 8 could be easily taken home to play with members of the family. The word rolls on Worksheet 7 could be used at home and some more words could be made up, helpfully leading to plenty of fun with silly non-words.

The coded alphabets on Worksheets 15 and 28 could be brought home and family members could decode secret messages made up at school.

To go with Worksheet 22 children could be asked to involve their parents in making up little two-line poems with pairs of rhyming words and either just memorise them or write them down – a prize for the snappiest, funniest, silliest, shortest?

To accompany the activity on Worksheet 26 children could compose other wh- questions to ask of their family members and bring back answers either orally or written.

And finally – don't forget that valuable home practice can be achieved not just with adult family members but also with siblings or cousins.

1

Underline the word that matches each picture.

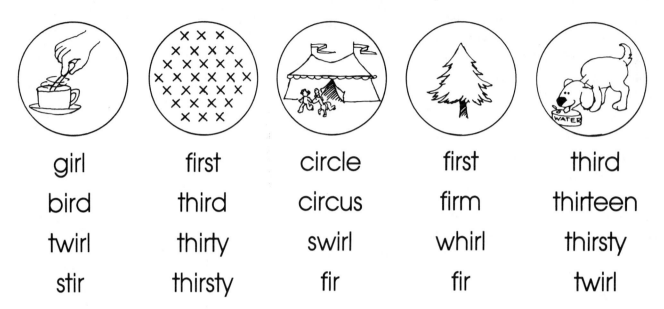

girl	first	circle	first	third
bird	third	circus	firm	thirteen
twirl	thirty	swirl	whirl	thirsty
stir	thirsty	fir	fir	twirl

Underline the sentence that matches each picture.

The girl is third in line.
The dog is thirsty.

The boy tore his shirt.
A wheel is shaped like a circle.

Write down all the **ir** words you find in this picture puzzle.

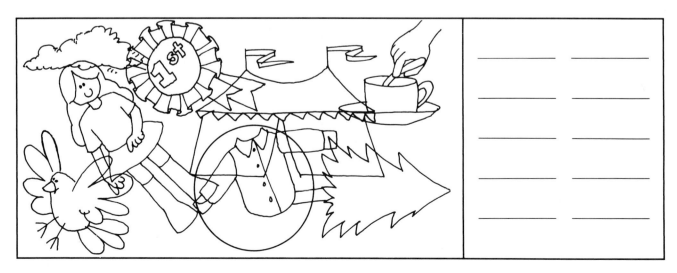

2

Fill the gaps with **ir** words to finish the story.

thirsty   girl   dirty   skirt   shirt

The children were playing in the garden.
The ground was very muddy after the heavy rain
and their clothes got very _____.
When their mum called them for tea
she told them to change their messy clothes.
The _____ changed her _____
and her brother put on a clean _____.
Then their mum gave them a drink because they
were _____.

Now draw four pictures to show the story.

3

Find the **ir** and **oo** words in the picture.
Circle the words you find in the list below.
Then colour in the picture.

hoop	roof	spoon	bird	skirt
moon	root	bloom	girl	shirt
room	hoot	shoot	first	thirst
pool	cool	broom	dirt	
zoo	loop	school	third	

4

HIDDEN WORDS
As you find the words in the puzzle, cross them off the list.
Look down and across the puzzle.

a	b	o	o	t	c	d	e	s	w	o	o	p	f
g	r	h	i	o	j	k	l	m	n	o	p	o	q
r	o	s	t	o	u	v	w	x	y	z	a	o	b
a	o	b	s	t	o	o	l	c	d	e	f	l	g
h	m	s	c	h	o	o	l	i	j	s	o	o	n
k	l	m	n	o	p	q	o	r	s	p	t	u	v
w	x	y	z	a	b	c	o	d	e	o	f	g	h
i	j	k	d	r	o	o	p	l	m	o	n	o	s
p	q	r	s	o	t	u	v	w	x	n	o	o	n
y	z	a	b	o	s	c	e	f	g	h	i	j	o
g	l	o	o	m	k	l	m	n	s	o	p	q	o
o	o	r	s	o	t	u	v	w	t	r	o	o	p
o	o	a	b	o	c	d	e	f	o	g	h	i	j
s	m	k	l	n	m	n	o	p	o	q	z	v	s
e	t	u	v	w	x	y	z	s	p	o	o	k	a
b	c	d	e	f	g	h	i	p	j	k	o	l	m
a	b	l	o	o	m	o	p	o	q	r	s	a	z
b	c	d	e	f	g	h	i	o	j	k	l	m	o
n	o	p	q	r	f	o	o	l	s	t	u	v	o

bloom
gloom
noon
soon
stoop
boot
goose
pool
spook
swoop
broom
loom
room
spool
tooth
droop
loop
school
spoon
troop
fool
moon
snoop
stool
zoo

5

e

Word wheel with segments: hat, can, cap, pal, mat, pan, tap, mad

WORD WHEEL
1. Cut out the word wheel.
2. Cut out the strip with the magic silent **e**.
3. Put the strip under the wheel so that the 2 black dots touch.
4. Make a hole through the black dots with a pin.
5. Put a paper fastener through the hole.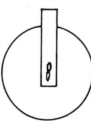
6. It should look like this.
7. Move the silent **e** strip around the wheel to make words.

How many words can you make? Write the words down and draw pictures for them.

 pane

 pan

6

1. I go around a picture.
   I can be made
   of wood.
   I am a _ _ a _ e.

WHAT AM I?

2. I can be opened and shut.
   I am found in a fence.
   I keep things in or out.

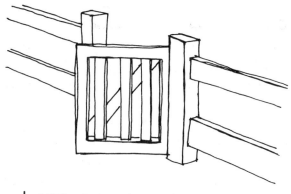

   I am a _ a _ e.

3. You put food on me.
   I am like a bowl,
   but flatter.

   I am the _ _ a _ e.

4. I am part of a car.
   You put your foot
   on me to stop.

   I am a _ _ a _ e.

5. I am part of a knife.
   I am not the handle.
   I am the cutting part.

   I am the _ _ a _ e.

6. I am something you play.
   Boys and girls like me.
   I am a _ a _ e.

Make your own **What am I** clues for these words.
Swap them with a friend to get the answers.

cave   slave   snake   lemonade   cake   tame

7

A	A	B	B
r	w	k	p
n	j	n	n
b	st	s	v
h	sm	b	t
s	cl	l	d
t	br	m	

MAKE A WORD MACHINE

1. Use a coloured pen to mark a cardboard roll into 4 parts.

2. Write a big **o** in the 2nd space.
   Write a big **e** in the 4th space.

3. Cut the four sound strips along the ____ lines.

4. Paste the ends together to make 4 little rolls.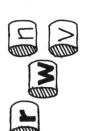

5. Slide one of the A strips in front of the **o**.
   Slide one of the B strips in front of the **e**.

6. Turn the sound strips around to make words.
   List all the words you make.

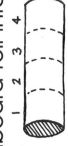 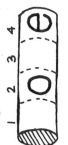  

8

HELP POOCH HOME!

Number of players 2   **you will need** 1 dice, 2 counters

How to play

Throw the dice and move the number of paces it shows.

Say the word you land on.

Make up a sentence using the word or act the word out.

If you don't know a word, miss a turn.

9

Draw lines to join the pictures with the correct words.

| dice | slide | pile | rice | nine | wine |
| time | smile | kite | five | hive | bike |

Draw lines to join each word to its correct meaning.

mice	the sun does this
ripe	the opposite of narrow
pile	belonging to me
shine	ready for eating
slide	the plural of mouse
kite	a stack of something
wide	for playing on at the park
mine	I fly when there is wind
hive	a home for bees

Use the pictures to help you name the rhyming words.
Then fill in the crossword below.

ACROSS

1. This word rhymes with **soot**.

2. This word rhymes with **look**.

3. This word rhymes with **brook**.

4. This word rhymes with **stood**.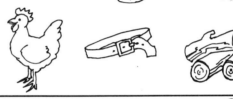

DOWN

5. This word rhymes with **took**.

6. This word rhymes with **good**.

7. This word rhymes with **full**.

Read the word, then make a new **ai** word. For example: **paid/laid**.

grain   rail   pain   faint

b ____   t ____   r ____   p ____

Follow the trail and write an **ai** word for each clue.

START — b _____

You think with this.

w _____

The middle of your body.

r _____

Water falling from the sky.

p _____

To give money in return for something.

n _____

The hard part on the end of a finger.

a ___

To help someone.

b _____

When you hurt.

p _____

You put this on a hook to catch fish.

m _____

The postman brings this.

h _____

Frozen rain.

FINISH

Magic Gold Paint

12

r ___ n   b ___ t   s ___ l

f ___ l   l ___ d   m ___ d

br ___ n   w ___ st   tr ___ n

Fill the gaps with **ai**. Then draw —

a snail and its trail	a long train
a grass stain on a shirt	a maid with a pail	bait on a hook

Write each word in a question.
For example: **train** — What time did you catch the train?

afraid _____

brain _____

trail _____

Underline the **oa** in each word.
Then write the words in alphabetical order.

| boat | roast | loaf | soak |
| foal | goat | toad | oak |

1. _____   2. _____   3. _____   4. _____

5. _____   6. _____   7. _____   8. _____

Finish these word puzzles by making **oa** words.

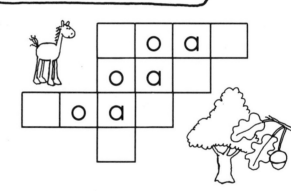

Draw this silly picture.
The toad in a red cloak ate toast
while floating in a boat in the moat.

14

Answer these sentences with **yes** or **no**.

A boat can float by the coast. _____

I can eat hot toast with a roast. _____

Mum soaks my clothes in soap. _____

Trucks can carry a load of coal. _____

Greedy goats eat coats and boats. _____

"Croak, croak," cries the toad. _____

Draw these things on the picture.

2 toads sitting on the rocks.
A goat eating grass on the hill.
A foal galloping along the coast.
4 oak trees by the road.
A load of coal in the boat.

●	□	▯	⌒	◓	◆	△	▤	▼	■	◇	◐	◨
a	b	c	d	e	f	g	h	i	j	k	l	m

★	▪	⇔	▤	△	∽	⩫	▦	◆	••	♡	▦	▱
n	o	p	q	r	s	t	u	v	w	x	y	z

Use the code to write **ou** words.

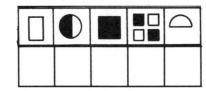
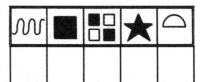

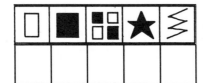
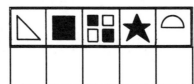
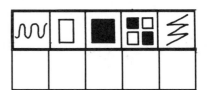

Can you crack this coded sentence?

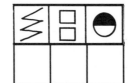
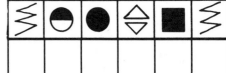

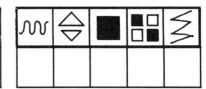

Write your own coded sentence. Swap with a friend to get answers.

16

Draw pictures in these boxes.
Then fill the crossword with **ou** words.

something round	An animal that lives underground.	something with a spout

1. Not **in**, but ____.
2. Not a **soft** sound, but a ____ sound.
3. Rain comes from this.
4. We use this to make bread and cakes.
5. A shape with no corners.
6. He likes to do good deeds.
7. A noise.
8. To say numbers in order — 1, 2, 3, ...
9. An animal's nose.
10. Belonging to us.
11. A hunting dog.
12. The earth — we stand on this.

17

MAKE A FLIP BOOK

1. Cut along the _____ lines.
2. Staple the pages together along the _____ lines.
3. Cut the .... lines.
4. Turn the word pages and the picture pages to match the words and pictures.
5. Add extra **or** words to your book.

cork	doctor	corn
horn	pork	stork

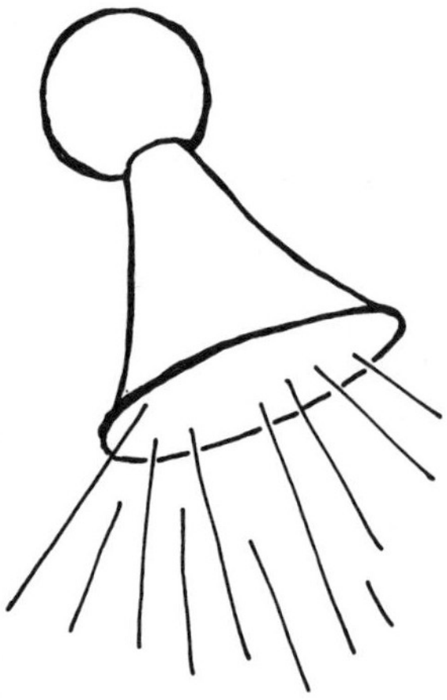

18

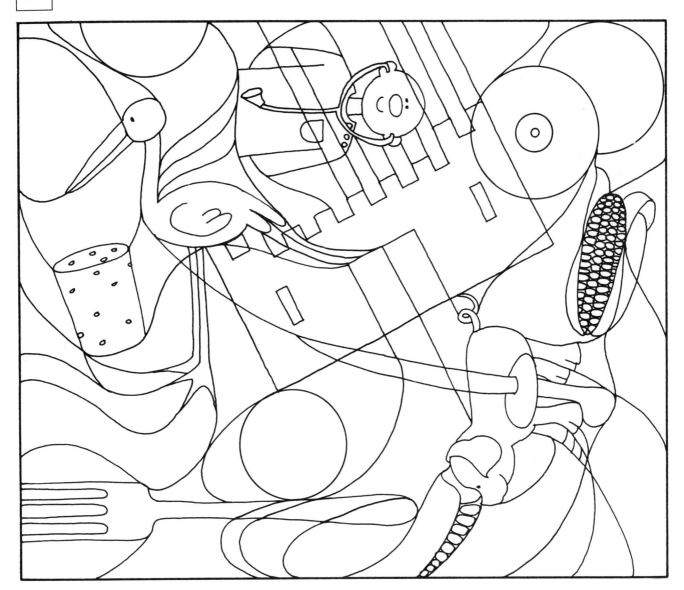

How many **or** words can you find in the jigsaw picture?
List them below, then colour them in.

_____ _____ _____ _____ _____

_____ _____ _____ _____ _____

19

how   fowl   flower
cow   gown   frown
now   down   growl
bow   brown shower
owl   meow

WHAT AM I?

1. I am the colour of nuts and wood.
2. I am a farm animal. I give milk and I eat grass.
3. I grow on most plants. I have petals. Seeds grow in me.
4. I am a farm bird. Ducks, hens and geese have this name.
5. I am the opposite to **up**.
   I am also soft feathers on a duck's chest.
6. I come on to your face when you are unhappy or thinking hard.
7. We do this when we meet the Queen.
8. You turn me on to wash yourself. I squirt water through a nozzle.
9. I am a bird with big eyes. I hunt at night. I eat mice.
10. Write your own **What am I** for **gown**.

10. g o w n

_____

_____

20

Fill the gaps to make **ow** words.
Then list the words in alphabetical order.

d __ __ n   br __ __ n   1. _____   4. _____

t __ __ el   gr __ __ l   2. _____   5. _____

h __ __ l   cl __ __ n   3. _____   6. _____

Answer **yes** or **no** to each question. Then write 2 **yes** or **no** questions in the space below. Swap with a friend to get the answers.

1. Do funny clowns have sad faces? _____

2. Is a sow a male pig? _____

3. Are all cows brown? _____

4. Can a dog growl? _____

_____

_____

21

To climb the stairs, write the **air** word that answers the **What am I** question next to the correct number.
Then write your own **What am I** for **pair** below.

1. You do me to things that are broken. Another name for me is **mend**.
2. We are things that you climb. Another name for us is **steps**.
3. I am small and magic. I have wings and a wand.
4. I am fun. I have games, rides and stalls.
5. I can be long or short, straight or curly. You can cut me.
6. I am invisible. I am all around you. You breathe me.
7. I am at the top of the stairs. I am opposite to **downstairs**.

pair _____

FIND THE aw WORDS
Draw lines to divide the letters into words.
Then write the words in the spaces below.

draw/clawpawstrawrawjaw

draw ____ ____ ____ ____ ____

sawlawncrawlhawkbawldawn

____ ____ ____ ____ ____ ____

prawnsawndrawnbawlsprawllaw

____ ____ ____ ____ ____ ____

Now draw these pictures.

a bawling baby	a hawk on a lawn	a cat's paw with claws

23

SOLVE THE CLUES
Answer each clue with an **aw** word.
Then write a story using the **aw** words below.

A dog's foot is a _____ .

Another name for sunrise is the _____ .

Something not cooked is _____ .

A tool for cutting wood is a _____ .

A part of your mouth that moves is your _____ .

A sharp nail on an animal's foot is a _____ .

When you make a picture you _____ .

lawn   crawl   bawl   saw   strawberry

_____

_____

_____

FINISH THE RHYMES
Find an **ow** word to finish each rhyme.

1. The grass has **grown**. It must be _____.

2. The seeds I have **sown** have _____.

3. Can you see the **snow** through the _____.

4. The water will **flow** _____ the bridge.

5. I used a trailer to **tow** the horses to the _____.

6. A strong wind will _____ away the **snow**.

7. As the sun sank **low** the moon began to _____.

mown   low
slow   glow
below   window
show   grown
sown   blow

25

WORD FAMILIES
Circle the odd one out, then write it in the space.

1. blow   blown   snow   _____
2. grow   crow   grown   _____
3. mow   mown   blown   _____
4. slow   sow   sown   _____

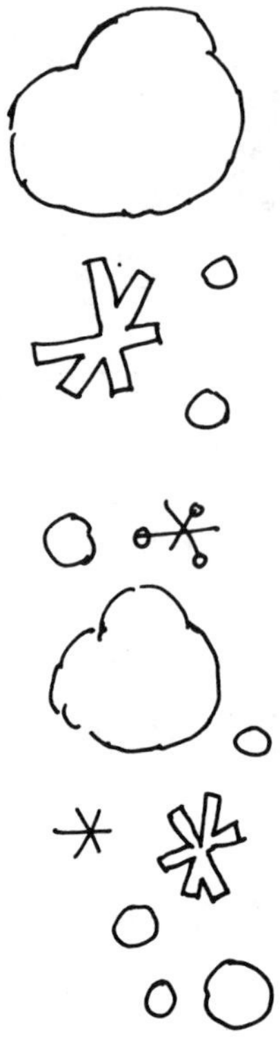

Where do snowflakes dance? At the snowball!

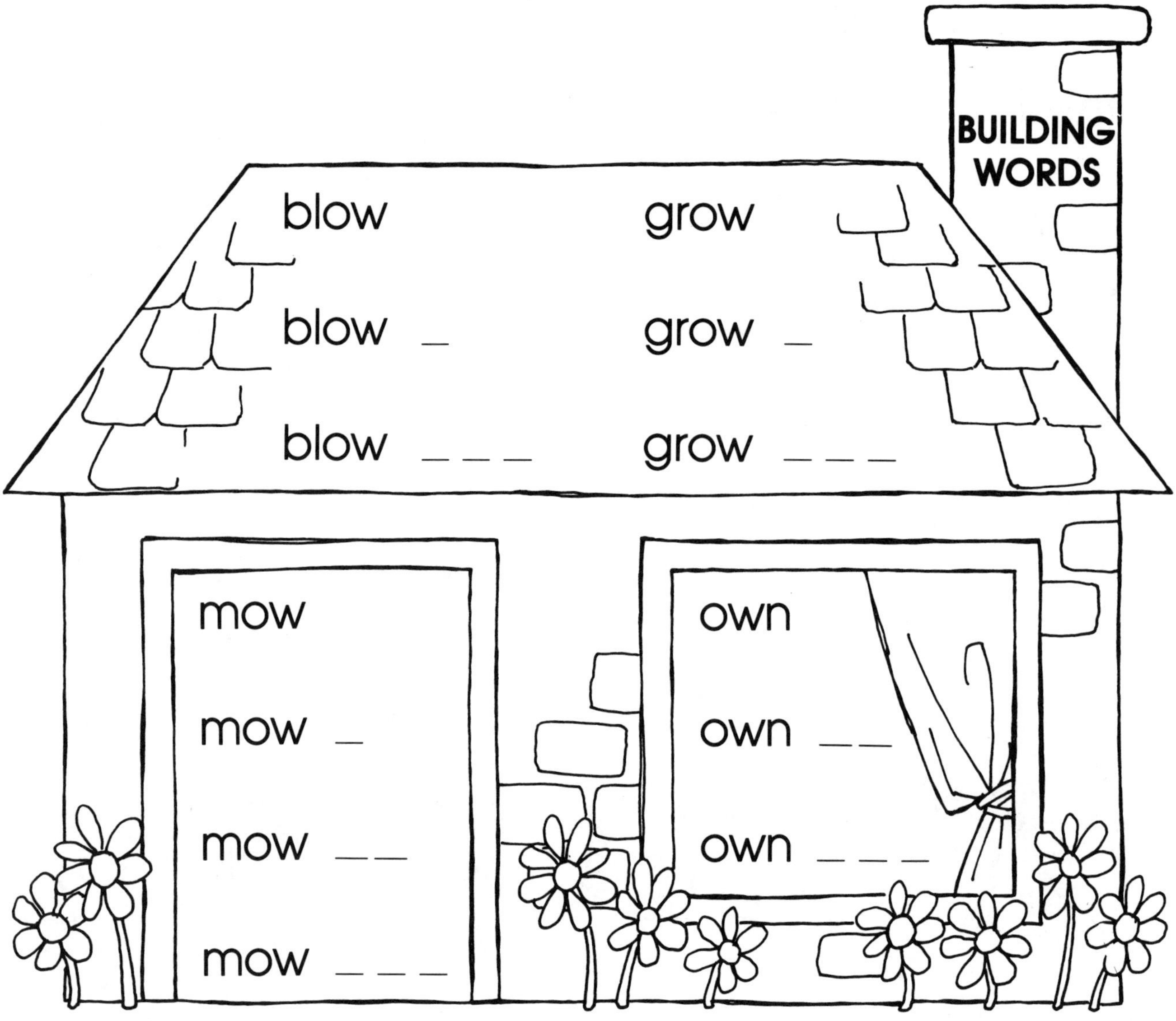

BUILDING WORDS

blow   grow
blow _   grow _
blow ___   grow ___

mow   own
mow _   own __
mow ___   own ___
mow ___

26

Write a question for each of the answers. The first word has been given to you. Remember to use a question mark (**?**).

Q. Where _____
A. I have been to market.

Q. When _____
A. The bus came at 6 o'clock.

Q. Which _____
A. Mine is the blue coat.

Q. What _____
A. I would like that toy bear.

Now write an answer for each of the following questions.

Q. What is your name?   A. _____

Q. Where do you live?   A. _____

Q. When is your birthday?   A. _____

Q. Which is your favourite colour?   A. _____

Cut out these puzzle pieces and put them together to make a witch. Complete the **tch** words. Then paste your puzzle on another piece of paper and colour it in.

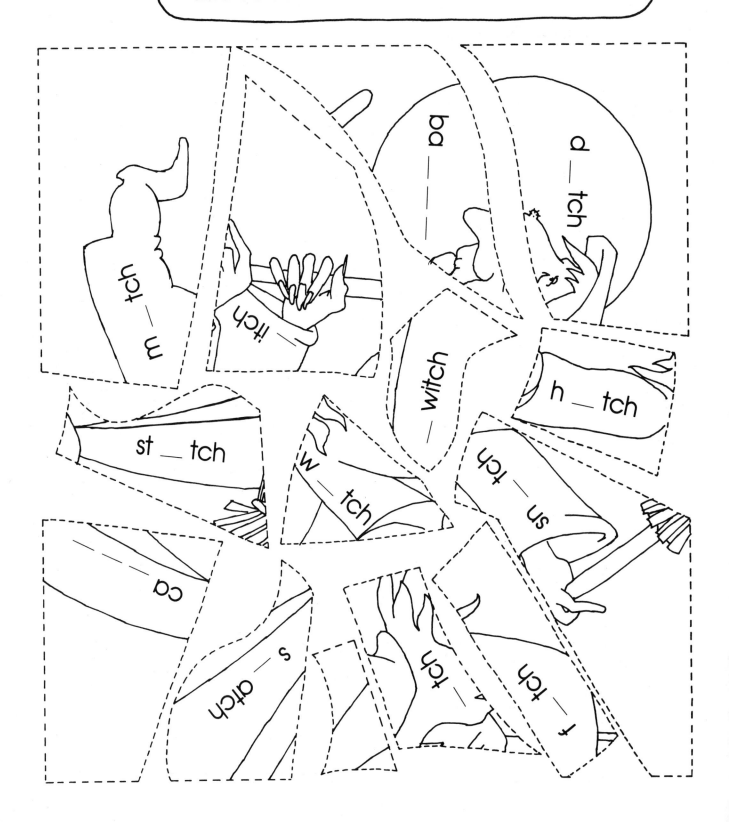

●	▢	▯	⌒	◓	◆	△	▤	▼	▮	◇	◐	◨
a	b	c	d	e	f	g	h	i	j	k	l	m

★	■	⬖	▭	◺	ﬡ	⚡	▨	◆	••	♡	▦	▱
n	o	p	q	r	s	t	u	v	w	x	y	z

Use the code to write these words.

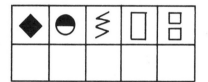

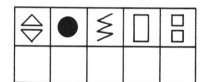

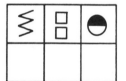
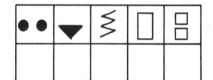

Can you crack this coded sentence?

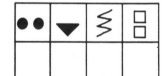

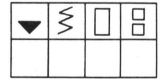
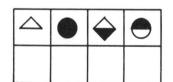

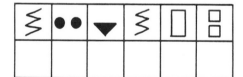

Now write your own coded sentence.

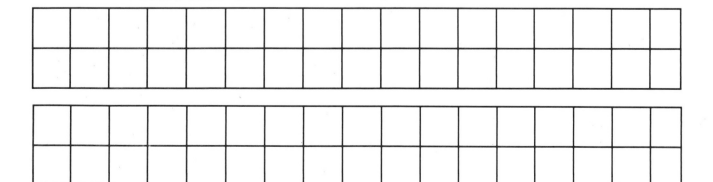

29

MAKE A WORD BASKET

How many **a** words can you write on the sides of the basket?

1. Cut around the solid lines.
2. Fold up the sides along the broken lines.
3. Fold down the tabs along the dotted lines and paste them inside the basket.
4. Make a handle from stiff card.

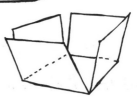

basket

as __

ca __ k

__ ath

fath __

bl __

a

cra __

m __ k

__ ft

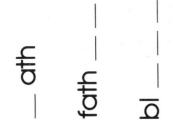

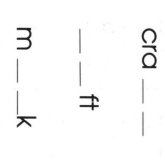

__ s __ v

__ s __ d

__ s __ l

WHAT AM I?

1. You have ten of me.
   I am found on your hand.
   I am a _ _ _ _ er.

2. I am hot and sunny.
   I come after spring.
   I am a season.
   I am _ _ _ _ er.

3. I flow between two banks.
   I carry water.
   I am a _ _ _ er.

4. I am a family member.
   I am female.
   I am the opposite to brother.
   I am a _ _ _ _ er.

5. I am a large group of animals.
   Cows and horses can be part of me,
   but ducks and sheep cannot.
   I am a _ er _ .

Make your own **What Am I** clues for these words.
(Write on the back of this sheet.)
Swap them with a friend to get the answers.

monster   under   farmer   clever

31

Cut out the words, then paste each word above the correct meaning.

leap	cream	real	creak	scream
				beak
leaf	bean	neat	mean	east
beach	beat	repeat	eat	least

a vegetable we eat	a loud noise	to jump	to chew and swallow food
a spooky noise	to do again	(leaf)	made from milk
very tidy	to hit	opposite to most	(beach)
opposite to west	unkind	(beak)	not made up

Follow the **ear** words to find your way out of the maze.
List the **ear** words you pass on the way.

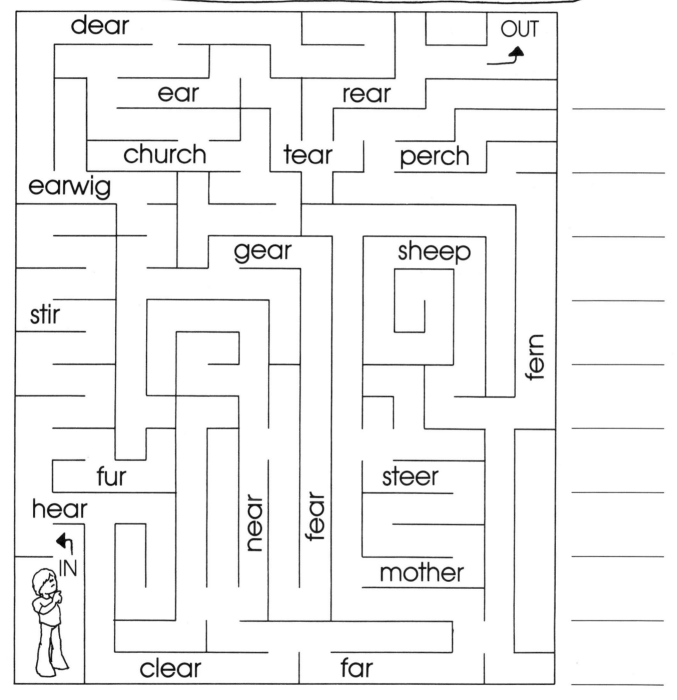

Now write a story about fear in 4 to 5 sentences, using as many of the listed **ear** words you can.
(Write on the back of this page.)

33

 Replace the pictures in the story with words from this list.
(*Shhh!* The **k** is silent.)

knit	kneel	knead	knocked
knee	knew	knight	knitting
knot	know	knife	knelt

The  in shining armour was told to

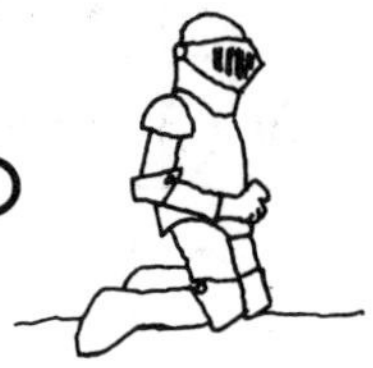

in front of the king. As he bent

his he  over the queen's

wool basket. She was cross as she got

a  in her  wool.

Draw the king's cook kneading bread dough.	Draw the knight slicing cheese with a knife.

34

Match each word in the top of the hour glass with its opposite in the bottom.
Then list the word pairs you have made.

Top of hourglass:
summer   midnight
today   early   sunset
autumn   night   dusk
afternoon   yesterday

Bottom of hourglass:
day   late
spring   winter
morning   tomorrow
dawn   tonight
sunrise   noon

autumn/spring

____ ____
____ ____
____ ____
____ ____
____ ____
____ ____
____ ____
____ ____
____ ____

How many other time words can you think of?

hour _____ _____ _____

_____

Time flies!

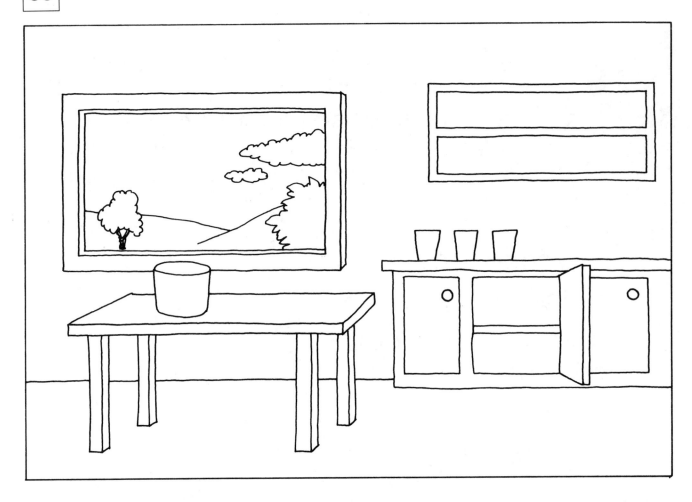

Complete this picture by carefully following the directions.

1. Put a mat **on** the floor.
2. Draw 3 flowers **in** the pot.
3. Colour the **middle** flower yellow.
4. Draw a clock on the wall **above** the window.
5. Draw some orange curtains on each **side** of the window.
6. Put a chair at the **end** of the table.
7. **Inside** the open cupboard draw 2 bowls.
8. On the **top** shelf on the wall draw 5 cups.
9. On the **bottom** shelf draw 4 jars.
10. Draw a fluffy cat **under** the table.
11. **Outside** of the house, draw the sun shining.
12. Draw a bottle of lemonade **beside** the glasses on the bench.

Now colour the picture in.

36

THE ALPHABET TRAIN

Cut out the engines and the carriages.
Then rearrange the trains in alphabetical order.

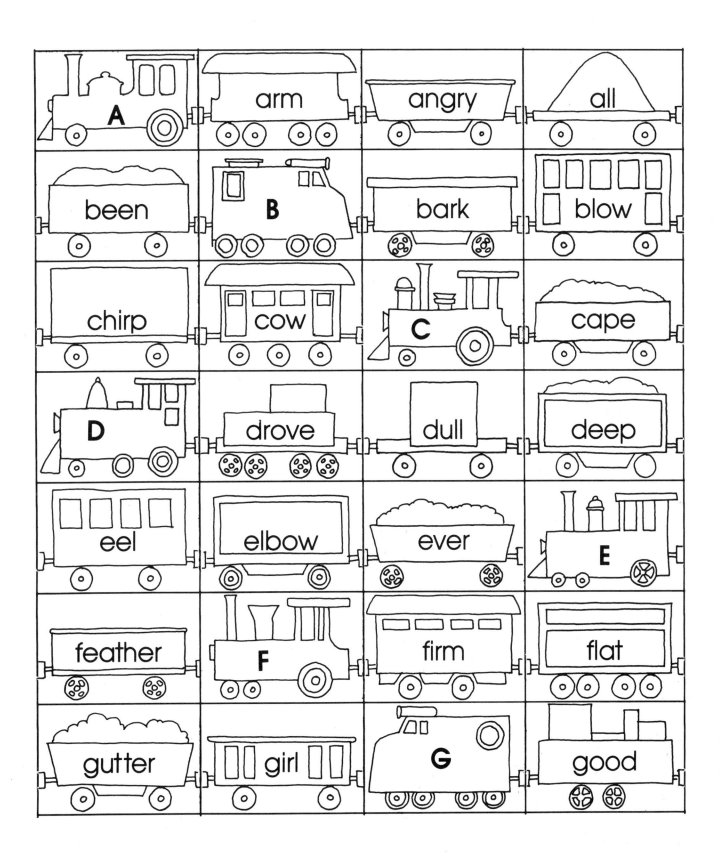

Can you change the letters around in these words to make new words? The meanings for the new words will help you.
Write the new word and draw a picture for it. The first one has been done for you.

ate ⟶ a drink ⟶ tea

pot ⟶ a toy that spins ⟶

ram ⟶ part of your body ⟶

tow ⟶ a number ⟶

end ⟶ a lion's home ⟶

pea ⟶ an animal ⟶

dear ⟶ what you do to a book ⟶

team ⟶ a kind of food ⟶

post ⟶ a dot ⟶

cork ⟶ a stone ⟶

felt ⟶ the opposite of right ⟶

Compound words are 2 small words joined together to make a bigger word, e.g.

fire + man = fireman

Make your own compound words.

1. Fold a piece of paper into 3 by bringing the 2 outside edges to meet in the middle. Your paper will have 2 equal doors that can be opened.

2. On the front of the doors write 2 small words that can be joined together to make a compound word, e.g. rain — bow. Draw a picture for each word.

3. Open up the 2 doors and write the compound word inside. Draw a new picture.

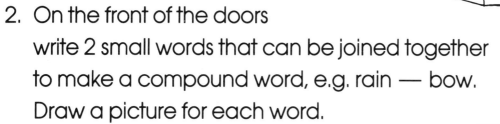

4. Try it with these words:
   hand — bag   light — house   tea — pot   sun — flower

Can you think of any more compound words?

_____   _____   _____   _____

_____   _____   _____   _____

Compound words are 2 small words joined together to make a bigger word — e.g. **wind** + **mill** = **windmill**.

Write the 2 small words beside each compound word.

without   _____ _____   myself   _____ _____

forget   _____ _____   nobody   _____ _____

afternoon _____ _____   doorbell   _____ _____

inside   _____ _____   newspaper _____ _____

anyone   _____ _____   highway   _____ _____

Write the compound words to match the picture puzzles.
Then colour in the pictures.

Teacher's checklist

Names	Recognises 'oo' within words	Is able to use wh- question words	Understands what opposites are	Understands the principle of magic 'e'	Can order words alphabetically	Is able to rearrange anagrams	Is increasingly aware of digraphs such as 'aw', 'ea' (one sound represented by two letters)	Is increasingly aware of diphthongs such as 'ai', 'ow'	Is able to use longer letter strings (e.g. 'air', 'tch')	Can make and break compound words

Pupil's own checklist

Name .... Date ....

I can make up questions which start with a wh- word, like:

Wh ....

I know what magic 'e' is. Here are some words which have magic 'e':

.... e   .... e   .... e

I know what opposites are. Here are some pairs.

hot ....   dark ....

I can make three new words by putting together these old ones:

black   shade   ....
   step   lamp   ....
foot   board   ....

Here are some words that would follow each other in the dictionary:

....

....